Easy Adult Coloring Book

for good vibes

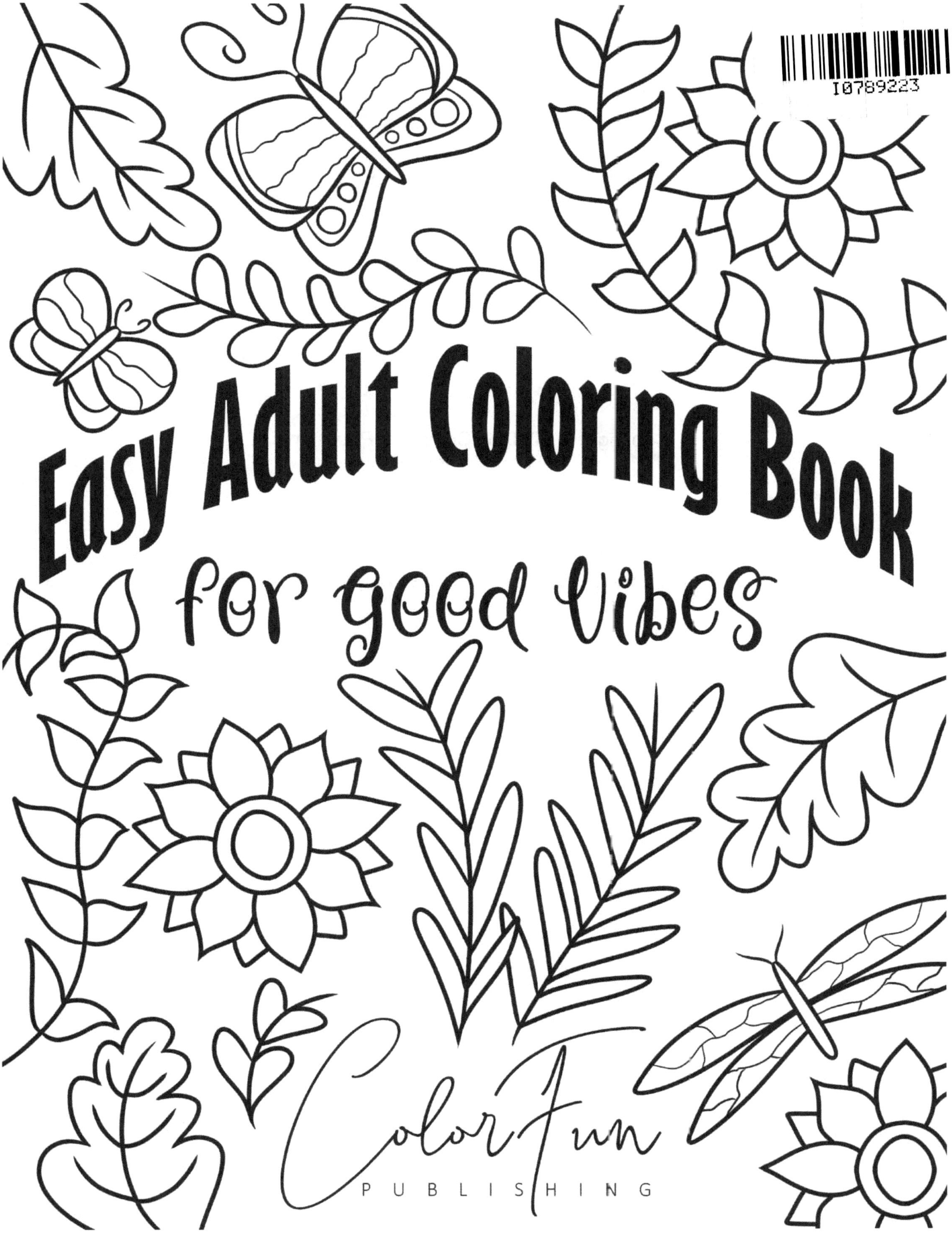

ColorFun
PUBLISHING

This book belongs to

Coloring Tips For You

Experiment different tools for coloring:
crayons, colored pencils, markers, fine tip pens, pastels, etc.
You can even mix different tools on images to see what works best for you.
Remember the spirit: Have Fun!

Before you start, test your tool on the coloring test page.
This little move will make sure a great start on your coloring work.

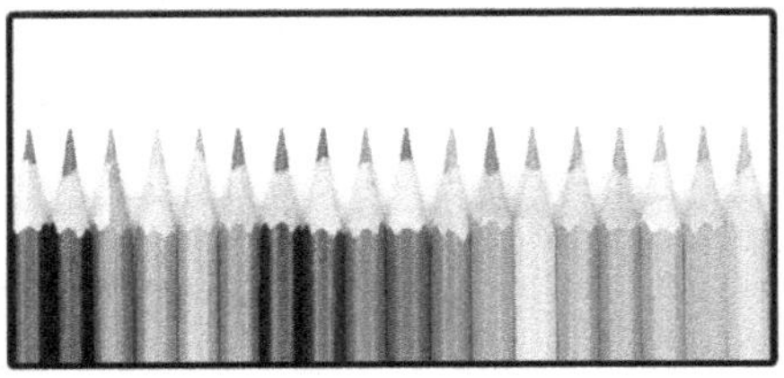

When using colored pencils, make sure they are sharp so that you can cover small areas or fine details with ease.

When using colored pencils, crayons or pastels, start out light!
You can always go back and darken your colors.

If you're using markers, it's highly recommended that you slide a thin paper or cardstock behind the pages you're working on. This tip is to prevent bleed-through.

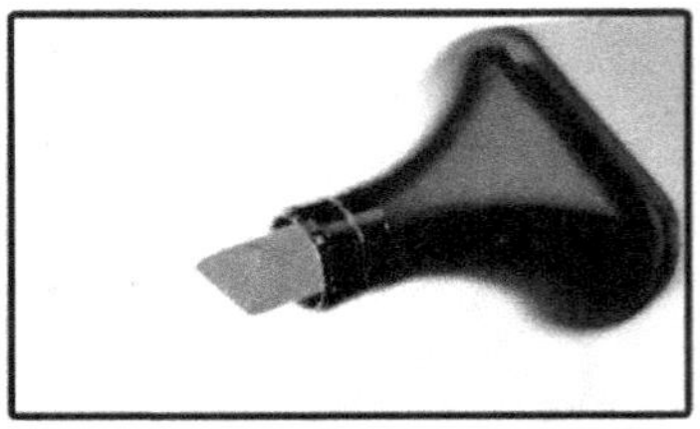

Follow your instinct! You can start on any image of your choice and pick up any color you feel like at that particular moment for your coloring work.
Make sure it's a precious process that allows inner talk!

Perfection is NOT the goal! Enjoy coloring and let your creativity go wild.
After finishing this coloring book, go back and see how your creativity has evolved over the images.

HAVE A GREAT TIME COLORING!

ColorFun
PUBLISHING

Color test page

Love
for
All

Am Strong

Die with
memories,
not dreams

What we
think,
we become

I LOVE
MYSELF

Change
the
Game

IT IS ON

It is well

SEE
THE
GOOD

Change
to be
kind

DONT
QUIT

IF YOU
WORK,
IT WILL
WORK

I AM HAPPY

PROGRESS,
NOT
PERFECTION

GO WILD
FOR
A WHILE

I CAN
AND
I WILL

You matter

NORMAL
IS
BORING

YOU ARE
ENOUGH

Be a voice.
Not an acho

WiTH YOU,
iT'S DiFFERENT

LEAN IN

I MISS YOU

PROVE
THEM
WRONG

Focuse on the good

MORE
SELF
LOVE

Pause
and reset

FAITH.
HOPE.

BEGIN
AGAIN

KEEP
GOING

Small steps
every day

ENJOY
IT
ALL

TAKE
CHANCES

SMILE

BE YOU

Be in
the
now

FIND
YOUR
FIRE

JOY

ALWAYS
BE KIND

Grow
gratitude

Love
vithout
limits

STAY TRUE

BE BRAVE.
BE BOLD.
BE YOU

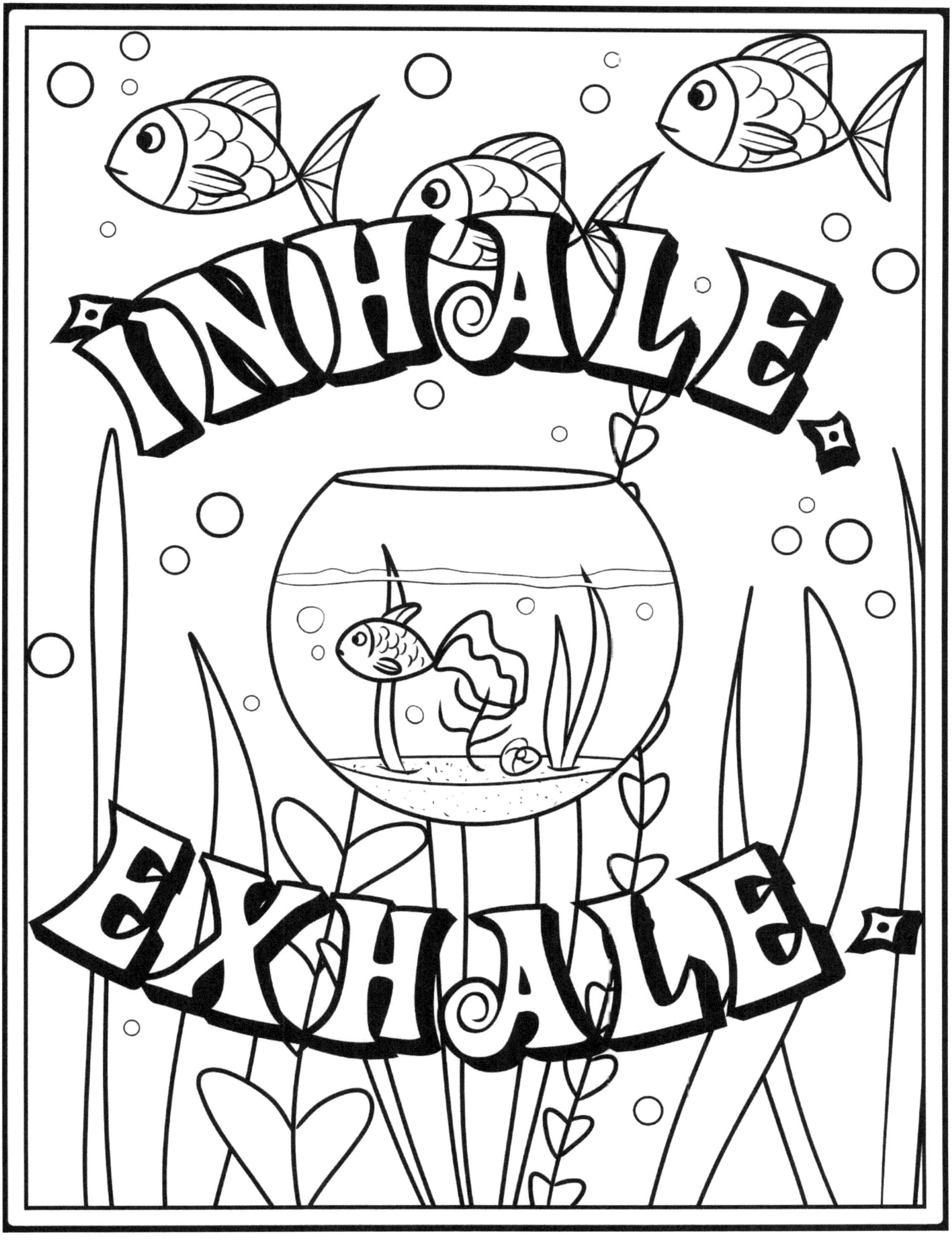
INHALE.
EXHALE.

DANCE. LOVE.
SING. LIVE.

DO IT
WITH
LOVE

Youg.
Old.
JUST WORDS

GOOD
JOB

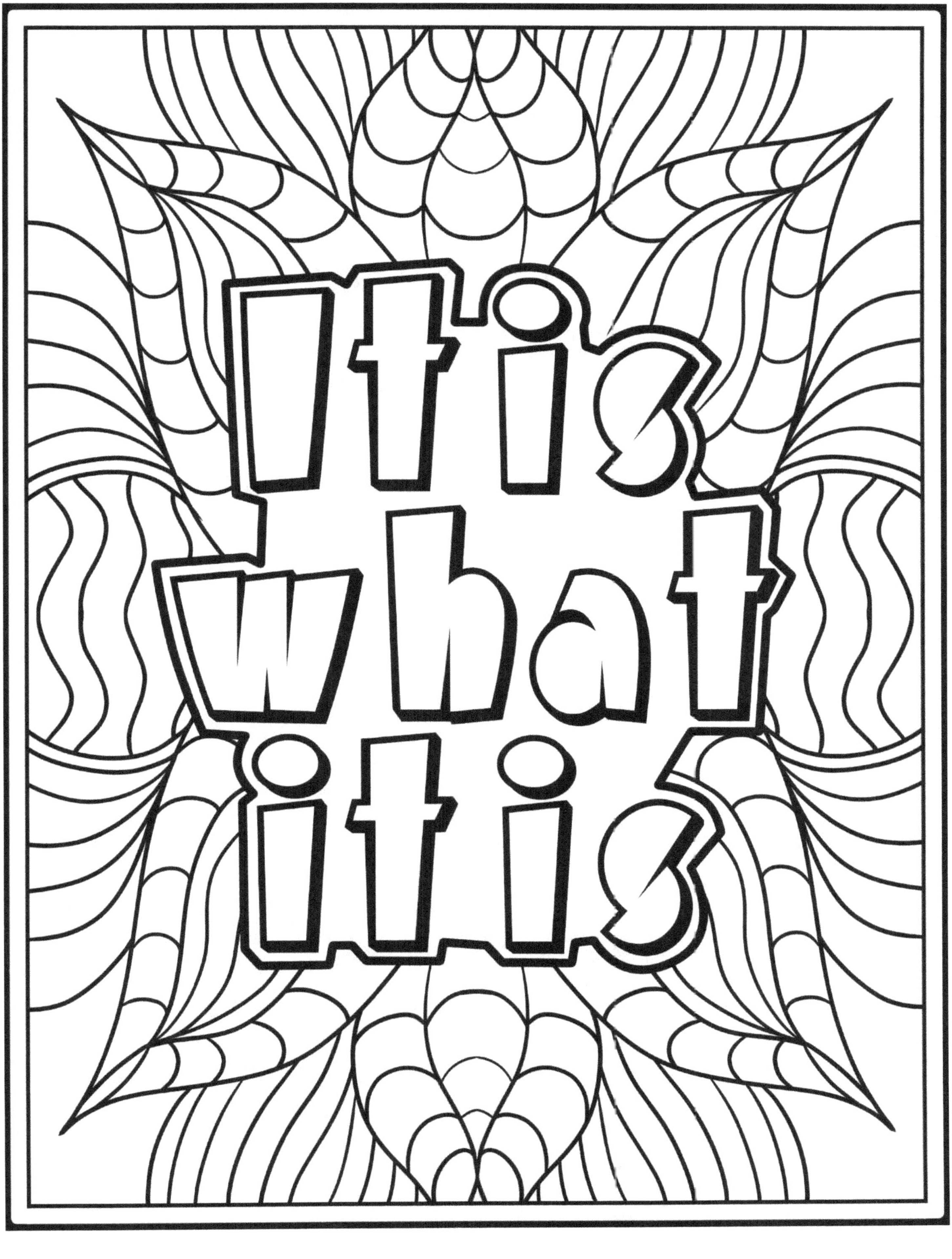
It is
what
it is

FEEL
YOUR
HEARTBEAT

Hey, it's not finished yet!

How's your coloring journey?
Do you have fun with this coloring book?
Friends or families you gave this book to like this book?

As fellow colorists, we really want to know your thoughts on this book. With your feedback, we'll be able to bring you more surprise with our next books.

So, PLEASE HELP!

Help leaving helpful comments and rating on the website where you found us.
Your comments and rating would definitely benefit others.

Meanwhile, you can share your work with us!
By sending your work to colorfunpublishing@gmail.com, you'll get FREE digital copy of this coloring book.

That means, you can re-work on some of your favorite pages again!

Thank you again, and look forward to seeing your fantastic coloring work!

ColorFun
PUBLISHING

www.ingramcontent.com/pod-product-compliance
Lightning Source LLC
Chambersburg PA
CBHW081418250726
48654CB00013B/1745
* 9 7 9 8 6 9 2 8 2 3 3 7 3 *